1 They love to snack

Some bears love honey so much they rip open trees to reach a beehive – and even lap up the bees. But bears don't stick to honey, they eat all kinds of food.

sun bear

SHOW YOU LOVE A BEAR
Don't tempt a hungry bear! Human food is not good for them so if you are camping in bear country, keep food out of the way.

From berries and bark to fish and meat, bears eat whatever they can find. Only giant pandas are different – they just chew on bamboo.

2 They build cosy dens

Bears make comfortable places to sleep. They dig out dens in hollows beneath tree roots or make nests in caves to escape the rain.

rain

den

forest floor

roots

Asian black bear

Some Asian black bears build day beds in trees while polar bears make dens in snowdrifts. Den-making bears like secret, quiet places where they can sleep in peace.

3 They can sleep for months

In winter, when it is difficult to find food, some bears go into a deep sleep to save energy. Hibernating in their dens, they can sleep for 100 days without eating and drinking. Their breathing slows down and their hearts hardly beat at all.

hillside

wildflowers

In spring, as the weather warms, bears wake up. Pregnant female bears give birth in their dens and only come out when there is enough food for their cubs to eat.

4 They give piggyback rides

A mother bear is loving and strict. She teaches her cubs all they need to know. Fiercely protective, she keeps them close. The cubs ride piggyback or are carried gently in their mother's mouth.

Bear cubs are full of mischief and endlessly curious. By watching their mother, these furry playmates learn to find food and keep safe. They may all stay together for as long as three years.

5 They wiggle and dance

Bears scratch their backs against trees to leave smells for other bears to find. By rubbing the bark, they post messages along their familiar forest trails. These marks may help them attract a mate or scare off a rival.

pine marten

cub

Most bears do a strange upright dance on their hind legs to leave their scent. But some giant panda bears aim higher and do a handstand to leave their mark!

6 They are terrific trackers

Bears have a much better sense of direction than humans. The polar bear is the greatest tracker of all. Like a mysterious compass in its shaggy head, instinct leads this wanderer home across the ice.

polar bear

seal pup

harp seal

With a sense of smell over 2,000 times better than ours, a bear can sniff food from 30 kilometres away. A polar bear can even smell the breath of a seal deep under the ice.

puffin

killer whale

7 They can surprise with a sprint

Bears look clumsy and slow. But an angry grizzly, a type of brown bear, sprints faster than a racehorse! Bears can run fast if they are hungry or cross. They can gallop uphill and downhill, but not for long. With their thick coats, bears quickly get hot and soon slow down.

They love a dip

Whether splashing around or having a soak, bears enjoy water. They paddle in lakes and rivers to escape biting insects, hunt for fish or cool off on hot days. But one bear swims to survive...

iceberg

The polar bear can swim hundreds of kilometres to find ice thick enough to hold its weight. It hauls itself out onto the ice to hunt, catching seals as they come up for air.

SHOW YOU LOVE A BEAR
Help stop climate change! Global warming is melting Arctic ice, so polar bears are forced to swim further and further to find food.

9 They hum in peace

From snorting and growling to grunting and coughing, bears make all kinds of noises that other bears understand. And if all is well, mother bears and their cubs just hum happily.

spectacled bear

bromeliad

Bears also use their bodies to show how they feel. They stand and stare, twist away, move their ears, sniff the air, charge forward or lie down and relax.

owl butterfly

clouds

prickly pear

SHOW YOU LOVE A BEAR

Make a noise about bears! Tell your friends some amazing bear facts so they learn to love them too.

10 They can be saved!

Living in remote forests in China, the giant panda is one of the rarest bears of all. This unusual bear bleats rather than growls and only ever eats bamboo.

giant panda